Introduction

In Pocket Money Christmas you will find lots of lovely projects for festive gifts, cards and decorations. They do not cost much to make and many of them use materials that you might have thrown away. Your pocket money will not only go a long way but you will also help the planet.

Have a look at pages 2-3 to see all the kinds of things you can keep to recycle. Old clothes, plastic bags and sweet wrappers are not rubbish at all! The symbol ☯ in the list of things for each project shows you where you can use them. There are also template shapes and simple instructions on how to use them on page 24.

Here's a guide to the star system used for each project:

★   very easy and quick.
★★   will take a bit longer.
★★★   more of a challenge.

Use good glue (but not superglue).

Make sure your pencils are sharp.

Use sharp, clean scissors.

Before you start on a project make sure you read it through and get everything you need ready. Work on a clean, flat surface with plenty of room. If you need to use scissors, knives, the iron or the oven do take care and have an adult standing by.

Treasure not Rubbish

Here is a selection of things you can keep to use for the projects in this book and for others too.

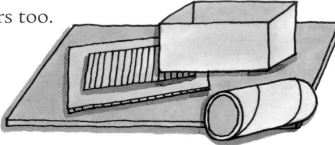

Old Woollens

Put old jumpers and other woollen clothing into the washing machine on the hottest wash. This will shrink them and produce a 'felty' effect.

Card, Cardboard Boxes and Tubes

Small, large, thick, thin and corrugated are all useful.

Plastic Bags

Keep thicker, coloured ones. It doesn't matter if there is writing or pictures on them.

Old Jeans

Wash them. It doesn't matter if they have some holes!

Sweet Wrappers

Keep jewel-coloured foils and cellophane.

Scraps of Material

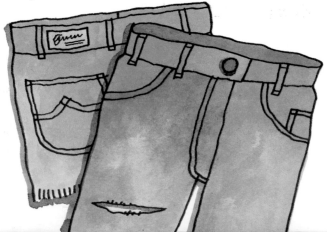

Giftwrap, Tissue Paper and Greetings Cards

Save old paper and smooth it flat with a cool iron. Keep it flat or roll it up. Save old greetings cards you like.

Newspapers and Magazines

Large Plastic Bottles

Wash and remove any labels. See-through and coloured bottles are both useful.

Corks and Metal Tops

Rinse bottle tops and dry them.

Wire Coat Hangers

Buttons

Every colour and size.

Twigs, Fircones and Shells

Whilst on walks in the countryside, park or on the beach, pick up interesting natural objects.

3

Party Hats

Make these with your friends for a party or make some for each of the family to wear at the Christmas dinner.

Crown

❄ thick, coloured paper ↻
❄ sweet wrappers ↻
❄ scissors
❄ ruler and pencil
❄ glue
❄ sticky tape or stapler

Cut strips of paper 10 cm wide and 58 cm long.
Draw and cut a pattern along one side.

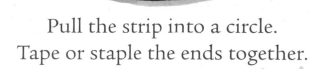

Pull the strip into a circle.
Tape or staple the ends together.

Glue on crumpled sweet wrappers to decorate.

Cone

✳ thick, coloured paper
✳ tissue or crêpe paper
✳ sticky tape or stapler
✳ 40-cm thin elastic
✳ ruler and scissors
✳ pencil and compass

← 29 cm →

Draw and cut out a semi-circle of paper.

Pull the paper round to form a cone. Secure with sticky tape.

Cut some tissue or crêpe paper into a 13-cm wide strip. Cut it into a fringe.

Cut a tiny bit off the point of the cone. Roll up the fringe and poke the uncut end inside the cone. Secure inside with tape.

Cut some narrower fringes. Roll them up and attach them to the cone with sticky tape or a staple.

Ruffle them with your fingers.

Tape the elastic inside. Wear with the elastic on the back of your head. Make the elastic longer if you want it to go under your chin.

Pillbox Hat

* thick paper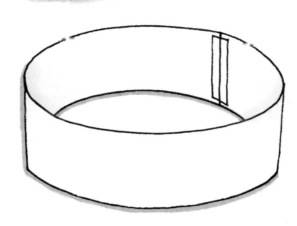
* crêpe and tissue paper
* sticky tape or stapler
* glue and scissors
* 40-cm thin elastic
* 2 rubber bands

Cut a strip of thick paper 6 cm wide and 48 cm long.

Join the ends with sticky tape or the stapler to form a ring.

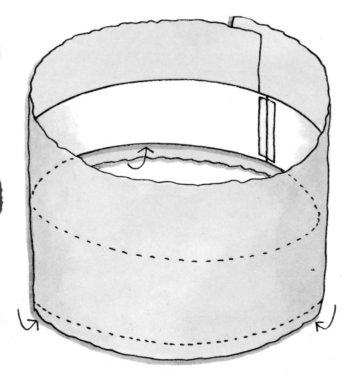

At the bottom, turn the crêpe paper a little up inside.

Cut the crêpe paper into a strip 21 cm wide and 51 cm long.

Glue this strip around the paper ring.

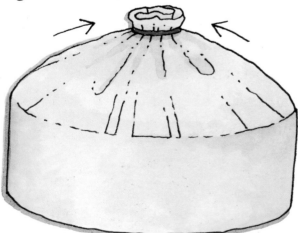

Draw the crêpe paper together in the centre and secure with a rubber band.

Cut different-coloured tissue paper into small fringes. Wind them around the gathered crêpe paper and attach them with the other rubber band. Fluff them out.

Attach the thin elastic to the inside of the hat. Wear with the elastic on the back of your head. Make the elastic longer if you want it to go under your chin.

Christmas Cake Hat

❄ white crêpe paper ↻
❄ giftwrap ↻

Make this like the Pillbox Hat but when you gather the paper into the centre on top, tape it flat.

Cut a strip of giftwrap the same size as the ring. Cut the long edges into fringes and tape around the ring.

Cut out the Christmas templates with flaps from page 24. Colour in and stick them on top.

Decorations

Paper Chains

❋ giftwrap 🔄
❋ ruler and scissors
❋ glue

Cut the giftwrap into strips
2.5 cm wide and 22 cm long.

Put glue on one end of the strip.
Form into a loop and glue to the
other end.

Loop a second strip into the first
and glue the ends together.

Carry on in this way to make a long chain.
Make lots and hang them up.

Christmas Tree Baskets

* stiff coloured paper
* patterned paper
* glue and sticky tape
* pencil and compass
* ruler and scissors
* wrapped sweets

Draw and cut out one circle of plain paper 4 cm in diameter and one a little smaller of patterned paper. Glue them together.

Cut a strip of coloured paper 1.5 cm wide and 20 cm long.

Roll the circle gently so it curves. Overlap the paper strip underneath and tape it in position. Lightly glue a wrapped sweet in the basket. Hang it on the tree.

Variations

Cut the circles with pinking shears.

Cut the circle edges into small fringes.

Fan Garlands

* tissue paper in two colours
* ruler and scissors
* glue
* stapler or sticky tape

Cut the tissue paper into strips 3.5 cm wide and 12 cm long.

Fold into a 2-cm wide concertina. Secure one end with a stapler or sticky tape.

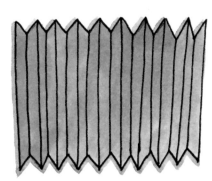

Make lots of fans in both colours.

Stick the fans together by gluing them along the outside edge.

Join each fan, alternating the colours, and with the ends alternating up and down.

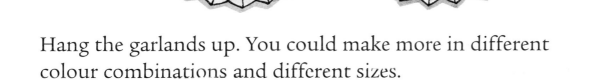

Hang the garlands up. You could make more in different colour combinations and different sizes.

Fantastic Circles

❄ coloured thread ♻

Make four fans as before, two in one colour, two in another.

Glue together along the outer edge, keeping all the ends in the centre.

Insert the end of a length of thread in the last glued edge and pull into a circle.

Hang it up.

11

Festive Food

Pinwheels

These little biscuits are perfect for a party.

Makes about 40

* ❄ 500 g ready-made puff pastry (thawed if frozen)
* ❄ 100 g strong Cheddar cheese, grated
* ❄ 2 tablespoons tomato purée
* ❄ pepper and salt

Roll out the pastry on a lightly floured board into a rectangle about 5 mm thick.

Spread the tomato purée over the pastry and sprinkle the cheese on top. Add pepper and salt.

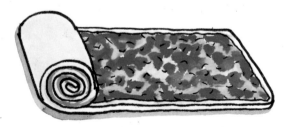

Roll up tightly and wrap in clingfilm. Put in the freezer for about two hours until firm.

Cut into very thin slices.

Place on a greased baking tray and cook for 10 minutes at 220°C/425°F. Serve warm.

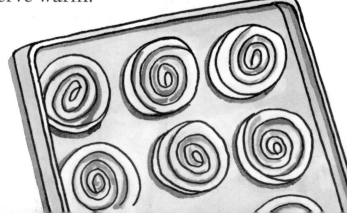

Christmas Biscuits

Use festive-shaped cutters for these. Hang on the tree with red and green ribbons.

Makes about 20

- ❄ 175 g softened butter
- ❄ 125 g granulated sugar
- ❄ 125 g soft light brown sugar
- ❄ 1 egg
- ❄ 350 g plain flour
- ❄ $1/2$ level teaspoon salt
- ❄ 1 level teaspoon cinnamon
- ❄ 1 level teaspoon ground ginger

Roll out on a floured surface to roughly 5 mm thick. Cut out Christmas shapes. Make a hole near the top with the end of a chopstick or similar.

Beat the butter and sugars in a large bowl until soft and fluffy. Gradually beat in the egg.

Fold the flour, salt and spices into the mixture. Beat it well then wrap in clingfilm and chill in the fridge for 30 minutes.

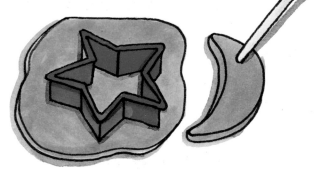

Place the biscuits on greased baking sheets. Prick lightly with a fork. Bake in the oven at 180°C/ 350°F for 12-15 minutes or until light brown.

Cool the biscuits on a wire rack.

Traditional English Trifle

This is a delicious pudding to make for a special occasion. Make it in a large glass bowl so you can see the pretty, colourful layers.

For 6 people

- ❉ 6 trifle sponges or plain sponge cake
- ❉ raspberry jam
- ❉ 225 g fresh raspberries or large tin raspberries, drained
- ❉ 50 ml fruit juice or juice from the tin
- ❉ 275 ml custard (see opposite)
- ❉ 275 ml double cream
- ❉ 50 g toasted flaked almonds

Slice the sponges or cake and spread with some raspberry jam.

Make them into 'sandwiches'. Place in the bottom of a large glass bowl.

Pour over the fruit juice or juice from the tin, if using. It should all soak into the sponges.

Sprinkle the raspberries on top.

14

Pour over the custard.
If it is warm leave it to cool.

Whip the cream until it is thick
but not stiff. Spoon it carefully
over the custard. Smooth the top.

Decorate the top with the
almonds. Cool the trifle in the
fridge before serving.

Homemade Custard

* 275 ml double cream
* 3 egg yolks
* 25 g caster sugar
* 1 level teaspoon cornflour

Heat the cream in a small saucepan.
Blend the egg yolks, sugar and
cornflour in a bowl very thoroughly.

Pour into the hot cream, stirring with
a wooden spoon over a very low heat
until thick. Do not let it boil.

15

Christmas Cards

Stained Glass Window

* coloured paper 21 x 15 cm
* old Christmas card
* pencil and tracing paper
* glue and scissors

Fold the coloured paper in half.

Trace the Stained Glass Window template from page 24. Then trace it on to the Christmas card so it frames a picture. Cut out the window shape.

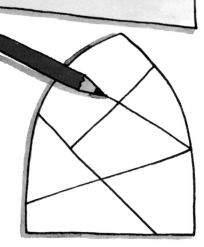

Turn it over. Divide it into seven pieces of roughly the same size.

Cut the pieces out and put them back together with the right side facing up.

Glue the pieces on to the card leaving a small space between each piece. Leave to dry.

Snowman

* coloured paper 21 x 15 cm
* white paper
* strip of fabric
* silver glitter
* felt-tip pens
* glue and scissors
* pencil and tracing paper

Fold the coloured paper in half. Trace the Snowman template from page 24 on to the white paper. Cut it out and glue it on the front of the card.

Draw the face and details.

Cut the fabric into a strip 17 cm x 2 cm.

Make a small hole on either side of the snowman's 'neck' with the scissors. Push the ends of the fabric through the holes from inside. Knot the ends together. Dab glue around the snowman and down his left side. Sprinkle with glitter.

Tree Decoration Card

Here a card and gift are combined. After Christmas remove the decoration and hang it on the tree next year.

* stiff coloured paper 21 x 15 cm
* scraps of fabric
* button
* thick card
* wool or thin string
* needle
* glue
* scissors
* pencil and tracing paper

Trace one of the Tree Decoration Card templates on page 24 on the thick card. Cut it out.

Place on the back of the fabric and draw around it. Cut out two, making them bigger than the outline.

Glue the fabric to both sides of the card shape with the right side of the fabric facing outwards.

Use lots of glue. If it soaks through it does not matter. It will dry and not show.

Hold firmly and cut a fine fringe all around the shape close up to it.

Ruffle the fringe with your fingers and make it fray a bit.

Thread a 25-cm length of wool or string on to the needle. Push it through the top of the card shape.

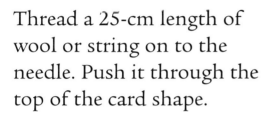

Pull into even lengths. Knot twice at the top to form a loop.

Fold the coloured paper in half to make a card.
Sew the button on to the top centre of the card.
Wind the loop around the button.

Variations

Glue sequins or small buttons on to the decorations.

Use different patterned fabrics for each side.

Use sparkly fabrics or brilliant silks. Tie on to bright, contrasting cards.

19

Gifts Galore

Everyone appreciates something different that has been specially made for them.

Festive Bookmarks

✳ old Christmas cards ↻
✳ red wool ↻
✳ ruler and pencil
✳ scissors
✳ hole punch (optional)

Tear the backs off the cards. Only use cards that have plain backs to the pictures. Cut into strips 15 cm x 5 cm.

Cut the bottom into a curve. Make a hole with the hole punch or point of the scissors.

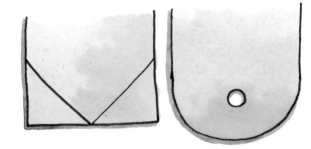

Write a message on the back.

Cut the wool into three 25-cm lengths. Fold in two and push the folded ends through the hole. Then push cut ends through the loop.

Glasses Case

- ❄ old woollen jumper ♺
- ❄ wool ♺
- ❄ button ♺
- ❄ needle and thread
- ❄ scissors and pins

Put the jumper into a hot wash. This will thicken and felt it. Leave it to dry and then cut a strip measuring 36 cm x 7 cm.

Cut one end into curve. Fold the other end.

Pin the sides and sew together with wool.

Sew a wool loop at the centre of the curved edge. Fold over and mark where to put the button. Sew it on.

21

Merry Mats

* 19 metal bottle tops ⟳
* scraps of cotton fabric ⟳
* compass and pencil
* scissors
* needle
* thread

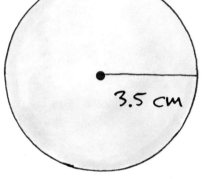

3.5 cm

Mark out 19 circles on the fabric.
Use the compass and pencil.
Cut them out.

Thread the needle with a double
length of thread. Sew a line of running
stitches around each circle of fabric.

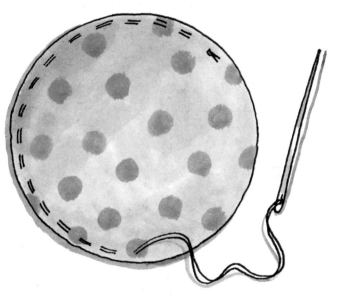

Place the bottle caps face down
on the wrong side of the fabric.
Continue the running stitch to
the end.

Pull the fabric tight around the
bottle tops. Secure it with a few
stitches. Cut off the thread.

Cover all 19 bottle tops in the same way. Arrange the tops in a pattern you like.

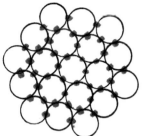

Turn the tops over and start sewing them together. Begin with the ones in the centre.

Sew a few stitches at the edges of the tops to join them together.

When they are all sewn turn the mat over!

More Mats

Make some smaller and larger mats.

Make a set of four or six drinks' mats.

Make a large round or oblong serving mat.

23

Template Shapes

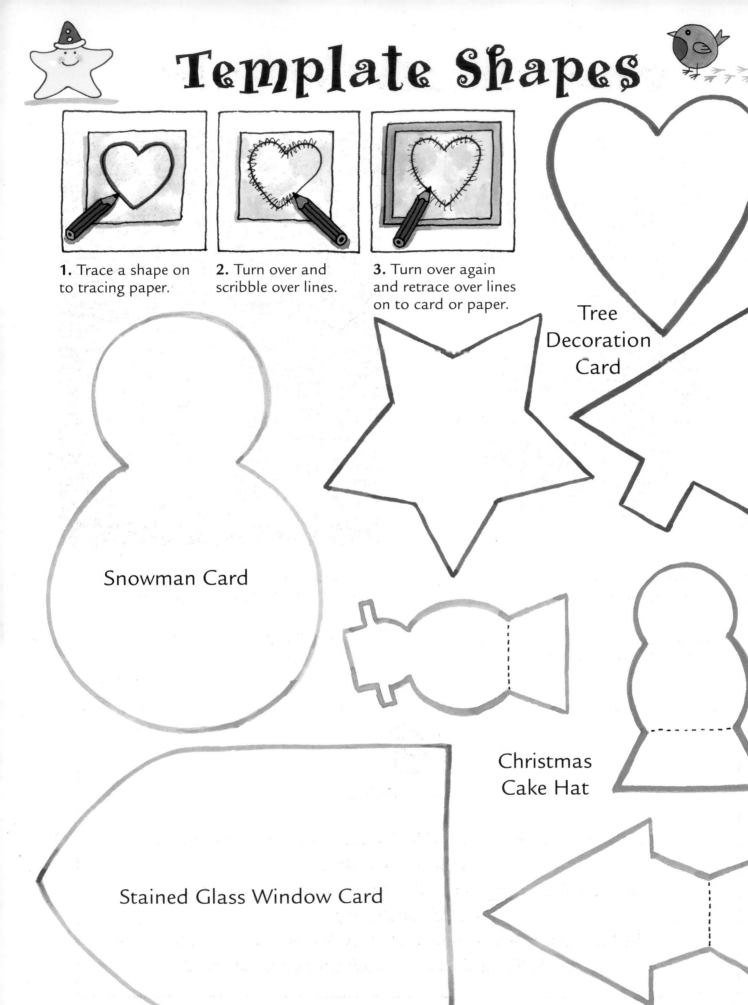

1. Trace a shape on to tracing paper.

2. Turn over and scribble over lines.

3. Turn over again and retrace over lines on to card or paper.

Tree Decoration Card

Snowman Card

Christmas Cake Hat

Stained Glass Window Card